# Once Upon a Christmas

Compiled by **Alice Gray**  Paintings by **Laurie Snow Hein**

BLUE COTTAGE GIFTS™
a division of Multnomah Publishers, Inc.
Sisters, Oregon

*Once Upon a Christmas*
Text © 2001 by Multnomah Publishers, Inc.
Published by Blue Cottage Gifts™, a division of Multnomah Publishers, Inc.
P.O. Box 1720, Sisters, Oregon 97759

ISBN 1-58860-047-5

Artwork © Arts Uniq'®, Inc.
Artwork designs by Laurie Snow Hein are reproduced under license from Arts Uniq'®,
Inc., Cookeville, Tennessee, and may not be reproduced without permission. For
information regarding art prints featured in this book, please contact:
*Arts Uniq'®, Inc.*
*P.O. Box 3085*
*Cookeville, Tennessee 38502*
*1-800-223-5020*

Designed by Koechel Peterson & Associates, Minneapolis, Minnesota

Multnomah Publishers, Inc., has made every effort to trace the ownership of
all poems and quotes. In the event of a question arising from the use of a poem
or quote, we regret any error made and will be pleased to make the necessary
correction in future editions of this book.

Please see the acknowledgments at the back of the book for complete
attributions for this material.

Scripture quotations are taken from *The Living Bible* © 1971. Used by permission of
Tyndale House Publishers, Inc. All rights reserved.
Printed in China

www.bluecottagegifts.com

# *Contents*

*May Christmas blessings on thee shine*
*And joy and peace be always thine.*

Anonymous

# Introduction

By Alice Gray

One by one, the rest of the family has finally drifted off to bed. It's almost midnight; I've waited for this quiet moment. With a long, contented sigh I settle deep into my favorite chair—and I am thankful. Tomorrow is Christmas.

The temperature outside has dropped below freezing. Light from a full moon and a million diamond stars transforms an earlier dusting of snow into silver frosting spread on tree branches. I snuggle into the warmth of the cream-colored throw my mother made years ago. This is my time to savor treasured memories.

I've always loved everything about the season: shopping malls decorated with ribbons and holly, searching for little gifts that celebrate relationships, the sights and smells and sounds that belong only to Christmas. But there's more to the season than the wrappings.

Christmas Eve for me meant family assembled in my mother's little house. Each year's gathering featured a crackling fire, twinkling poinsettia-shaped lights draped across the mantel, and scrumptious food only Mother could prepare, artistically arranged on the cherry wood dining table.

Woven through all the memories, Mother's lesson endures: Christmas was a birthday long before it was a holiday. Each year she created a fun way to teach that lesson. One year she held a treasure hunt for all the pieces of her Nativity scene; she'd carefully hidden them before we arrived. Another year, with the boys dressed in bathrobes and the girls with tinsel garlands in their hair, we were magically transformed into shepherds and angels as Mother read the Christmas story from her worn Bible. Still another year we wrapped warm socks and mittens, then delivered them personally to needy folks in the oldest part of town. Even the smallest child among us understood what Christmas was really about.

Christmas Eve always ended the same way. Though her hands were stiff with arthritis, Mother played Christmas carols on the organ Dad had given her after they bought their first and only home. Somehow her aged fingers still flew across the keys while delighted grandchildren danced to her lively renditions of "Jingle Bells" and "Frosty the Snowman." Eventually the music would slow. Our souls hushed and we eased into a quieter, almost sacred mood. We filled the house with reverence and joy for a manger, a silent night, and a message of peace on earth.

It's past midnight when I follow the rest of the family and slip quietly into bed. This time the contented sigh brings a knowing smile: *Today is Christmas.*

# Mrs. Hildebrant's Gift

By Robert Smith

*I*t's been thirty years since I last saw her, but in memory she's still there every holiday season. I especially feel her presence when I receive my first Christmas card.

I was twelve years old, and Christmas was only two days away. The season's first blanket of white magnified the excitement.

I dressed hurriedly, for the snow was waiting. What would I do first—build a snowman, slide down the hill, or just throw the flakes in the air and watch them flutter down?

Our station wagon pulled into the driveway, and Mom called me over to help with the groceries. When we finished carrying in the bags, she said, "Bob, here are Mrs. Hildebrandt's groceries."

No other instructions were necessary. As far back as I could remember, my mom shopped for Mrs. Hildebrandt's food and I delivered it. Our ninty-five-year-old neighbor who lived alone was crippled from arthritis and could take only a few steps with her cane.

Even though she was old, crippled, and didn't play baseball, I liked Mrs. Hildebrandt. I enjoyed talking with her; more accurately, I enjoyed listening to her. She told wonderful stories of her life—about a steepled church in the woods, horse and buggy rides on Sunday afternoon, and her family farm without running water or electricity.

She always gave me a dime for bringing her groceries. It got so that I would refuse only halfheartedly, knowing she would insist. Five minutes later, I'd be across the street in Beyer's candy store.

As I headed over with the bags, I decided this time would be different, though. I *wouldn't* accept any money. This would be my Christmas present to her.

Impatiently, I rang Mrs. Hildebrandt's doorbell. Almost inaudible at first were the slow, weary shuffles of her feet and the slower thump of her cane. The chain on the door rattled and the door creaked open. Two shiny eyes peered from the crack.

"Hello, Mrs. Hildebrandt," I said. "It's me, Bob. I have your groceries."

"Oh, yes, come in, come in," she said cheerfully. "Put the bag on the table." I did so more hurriedly than usual, because I could almost hear the snow calling me back outside.

As we talked, I began to realize how lonely she was. Her husband had died more than twenty years ago, she had no children, and her only living relative was a nephew in Philadelphia who never visited.

Nobody ever called on her at Christmas. There would be no tree, no presents, no stocking.

She offered me a cup of tea, which she did every time I brought the groceries. Well, maybe the snow could wait.

We sat and talked about what Christmas was like when she was a child. We traveled far away and long ago, and an hour passed before I knew it.

"Well, Bob, you must be wanting to play outside in the snow," she said as she reached for her purse.

"No, Mrs. Hildebrandt, I can't take your money this time. You can use it for more important things," I resisted.

She looked at me and smiled. "What more important thing could I use this money for, if not to give it to a friend at Christmas?" she asked, and then placed a whole *quarter* in my hand.

I *tried* to give it back, but she would have none of it.

I hurried out the door and ran over to Beyer's candy store with my fortune. I had no idea what to buy—comic books, chocolate, soda, ice cream. Then I spotted something—a Christmas card with an old country church in the woods on the cover. It was just like the one she'd described.

I handed Mr. Beyer my quarter for the card and borrowed a pen to sign my name.

"For your girlfriend?" he asked. I started to say no, but quickly changed my mind. "Well, yeah, I guess so."

As I walked back across the street with my gift, I was so proud of myself I felt like I had just hit a home run to win the World Series. No, I felt *better* than that!

I rang Mrs. Hildebrandt's doorbell. The almost inaudible sounds of shuffling again reached my ears. The chain rattled and the door creaked open. Two shiny eyes peered from within.

"Hello, Mrs. Hildebrandt," I said as I handed her the card. "Merry Christmas!"

Her hands trembled as she slowly opened the envelope, studied the card and began to cry. "Thank you very much," she said almost in a whisper, "Merry Christmas."

On a cold and windy afternoon a few weeks later, the ambulance arrived next door. My mom said they found her in bed; she had died peacefully in her sleep. Her night table light was still on, illuminating a solitary Christmas card.

*What brings joy to the heart is not so much the friends' gift as the friends' love.*

Saint Alfred of Rievaulx

# *Are you willing...*

*To stoop down and consider the needs*

*and desires of little children;*

*To remember the weakness and loneliness of people*

*who are growing old;*

*To stop asking how much your friends love you,*

*and ask yourself whether you love them enough;*

*To bear in mind the things that other people*

*have to bear in their hearts;*

*To trim your lamp so that it will give more light and less smoke,*

*and carry it in front so that your shadow will fall behind you;*

*To make a grave for your ugly thoughts*

*and a garden for your kindly feeling, with the gate open?*

*Are you willing to do these things for a day?*

*Then you can keep Christmas...*

*After all, Christmas-living is the best kind of Christmas-giving.*

HENRY VAN DYKE

# A Gift from the Heart

By Norman Vincent Pearle
Reprinted with permission from
January 1968 *Reader's Digest*

*N*ew York City, where I live, is impressive at any time, but as Christmas approaches, it's overwhelming. Store windows blaze with light and color, furs and jewels. Golden angels, forty feet tall, hover over Fifth Avenue. Wealth, power, opulence—nothing in the world can match this fabulous display.

Through the gleaming canyons, people hurry to find last-minute gifts. Money seems to be no problem. If there's a problem, it's that the recipients so often have everything they need or want that it's hard to find anything suitable, anything that will really say, "I love you."

Last December, as Christ's birthday drew near, a stranger was faced with just that problem. She had come from Switzerland to live in an American home and perfect her English. In return, she was willing to act as secretary, mind the grandchildren, do anything that was asked. She was just a girl in her late teens. Her name was Ursula.

One of the tasks her employers gave Ursula was keeping track of Christmas presents as they arrived. There were many, and all would require acknowledgment. Ursula kept a faithful record, but with a growing concern. She was grateful to her American friends; she wanted to show her gratitude by giving them a Christmas present. But nothing that she could buy with her small allowance could compare with the gifts she was recording daily. Besides, even without these gifts, it seemed that her employers already had everything.

At night, from her window, Ursula could see the snowy expanse of Central Park, and beyond it the jagged skyline of the city. Far below, in the restless streets, taxis hooted and traffic lights winked red and green. It was so different from the silent majesty of the Alps that at times she had to blink back tears of the homesickness she was careful never to show. It was in the solitude of her little room, a few days before Christmas, that a secret idea came to Ursula.

It was almost as if a voice spoke clearly, inside her head. "It's true," said the voice, "that many people in this city have much more than you do. But surely there are many who have far less. If you will think about this, you may find a solution to what's troubling you."

Ursula thought long and hard. Finally on her day off, which was Christmas Eve, she went to a great department store. She moved slowly along the crowded aisles, selecting and rejecting things in her mind. At last she bought something, and had it wrapped in gaily colored paper. She went out into the gray twilight and looked helplessly around. Finally, she went up to a doorman, resplendent in blue and gold.

"Excuse me, please," she said in her hesitant English, "can you tell me where to find a poor street?"

"A poor street, miss?" said the puzzled man.

"Yes, a very poor street. The poorest in the city."

The doorman looked doubtful. "Well, you might try Harlem. Or down in the Village. Or the Lower East Side, maybe."

But these names meant nothing to Ursula. She thanked the doorman and walked along, threading her way through the stream of shoppers until she came to a tall policeman. "Please," she said, "can you direct me to a very poor street…in Harlem?"

The policeman looked at her sharply and shook his head. "Harlem's no place for you, miss." And he blew his whistle and sent the traffic swirling past.

Holding her package carefully, Ursula walked on, head bowed against the sharp wind. If a street looked poorer than the one she was on, she took it. But none seemed like the slums she had heard about. Once she stopped a woman, "Please, where do the very poor people live?" But the woman gave her a hard stare and hurried on.

Darkness came sifting from the sky. Ursula was cold and discouraged and afraid of becoming lost. She came to an intersection and stood forlornly on the corner. What she was trying to do suddenly seemed foolish, impulsive, absurd. Then, through the traffic's roar, she heard the cheerful tinkle of a bell. On the corner opposite, a Salvation Army man was making his holiday traditional Christmas appeal. At once Ursula felt better; the Salvation Army was a part of life in Switzerland, too. Surely this man could tell her what she wanted to know. She waited for the light, then crossed over to him. "Can you help me? I'm looking for a baby. I have here a little present for the poorest baby I can find." And she held up the package with the green ribbon and the gaily colored paper.

Dressed in gloves and overcoat a size too big for him, he seemed a very ordinary man. But behind his steel-rimmed glasses his eyes were kind. He looked at Ursula and stopped ringing his bell. "What sort of present?" he asked.

"A little dress. For a small, poor baby. Do you know of one?"

"Oh, yes," he said. "Of more than one, I'm afraid."

"Is it far away? I could take a taxi maybe?"

The Salvation Army man wrinkled his forehead. Finally he said, "It's almost six o'clock. My relief will show up then. If you want to wait, and you can afford a dollar taxi ride, I'll take you to a family in my own neighborhood who needs just about everything."

"And they have a small baby?"

"A very small baby."

"Then," said Ursula joyfully, "I wait!"

The substitute bell-ringer came. A cruising taxi slowed. In its welcome warmth, she told her new friend about herself, how she came to be in New York, what she was trying to do. He listened in silence, and the taxi driver listened too. When they reached their destination, the driver said, "Take your time, miss. I'll wait for you."

On the sidewalk, Ursula stared up at the forbidding tenement—dark, decaying, saturated with hopelessness. A gust of wind, iron-cold, stirred the refuse in the street and rattled the reeling ashcans. "They live on the third floor," the Salvation Army man said. "Shall we go up?"

But Ursula shook her head. "They would try to thank me, and this is not from me." She pressed the package into his hand. "Take it up for me, please. Say it's from…from someone who has everything."

The taxi bore her swiftly from the dark streets to lighted ones, from misery to abundance. She tried to visualize the Salvation Army man climbing the stairs, the knock, the explanation, the package being opened, the dress on the baby. It was hard to do.

Arriving at the apartment on Fifth Avenue where she lived, she fumbled in her purse. But the driver flicked the flag up. "No charge, miss."

"No charge?" echoed Ursula, bewildered.

"Don't worry," the driver said. "I've been paid." He smiled at her and drove away.

Ursula was up early the next day. She set the table with special care. By the time she was finished, the family was awake, and there was all the excitement and laughter of Christmas morning. Soon the living room was a sea of gay discarded wrappings. Ursula thanked everyone for the presents she received. Finally, when there was a lull, she began to explain hesitantly why there seemed to be none from her. She told about going to the department store. She told about the Salvation Army man. She told about the taxi driver. When she was finished, there was a long silence. No one seemed to trust himself to speak. "So you see," said Ursula, "I try to do kindness in your name. And this is my Christmas present to you."

How do I know all this? I know it because ours was the home where Ursula lived. Ours was the Christmas she shared. We were like many Americans, so richly blessed that to this child there seemed to be nothing she could add to all the material things we already had. And so she offered something of far greater value: a gift from the heart, an act of kindness carried out in our name.

Strange, isn't it? A shy Swiss girl, alone in a great impersonal city. You would think that nothing she could do would affect anyone. And yet, by trying to give away love, she brought the true spirit of Christmas into our lives, the spirit of selfless giving. That was Ursula's secret—and she shared it with us all.

*How far that little candle throws his beams!*
*So shines a good deed in a naughty world.*

William Shakespeare

# Christmas in the Heart

It is Christmas in the mansion,

Yule-log fires and silken frocks;

It is Christmas in the cottage,

Mother's filling little socks.

It is Christmas on the highway,

In the thronging, busy mart;

But the dearest, truest Christmas

Is the Christmas in the heart.

Author Unknown

# A New Way to See Christmas

### By Gary Swanson

The mother sat on the simulated-leather chair in the doctor's office, picking nervously at her fingernails. Wrinkles of worry lined her forehead as she watched 5 year-old Kenny sitting on the rug before her.

He is small for his age and a little too thin, she thought. His fine blond hair hung down smooth and straight to the top of his ears. White gauze bandages encircled his head, covering his eyes and pinning his ears back.

In his lap he bounced a beaten-up teddy bear. It was the pride of his life, yet one arm was gone and one eye was missing. Twice his mother had tried to throw the bear away, to replace it with a new one, but he had fussed so much she had relented. She tipped her head slightly to the side and smiled at him. It's really about all he has, she sighed to herself.

A nurse appeared in the doorway. "Kenny Ellis," she announced, and the young mother scooped up the boy and followed the nurse toward the examination room. The hallway smelled of rubbing alcohol and bandages. Children's crayon drawings lined the walls.

"The doctor will be with you in a moment," the nurse said with efficient smile. "Please be seated."

The mother placed Kenny on the examination table. "Be careful, Honey, not to fall off."

"Am I up very high, Mother?"

"No dear, but be careful."

Kenny hugged his teddy bear tighter. "I don't want Grr-face to fall either."

The mother smiled. The smile twisted at the corners into a frown of concern. She brushed the hair out of the boy's face and caressed his cheek, soft as thistledown, with the back of her hand. As the office music drifted into a haunting version of "Silent Night," she remembered the accident for the thousandth time.

She had been cooking things on the back burners for years. But there it was, sitting right out in front, the water almost boiling for oatmeal.

The phone rang in the living room. It was another one of those "free offers" that cost so much. At the very moment she returned the phone to the table, Kenny screamed in the kitchen, the galvanizing cry of pain that frosts a mother's veins.

She winced again at the memory of it and brushed aside a warm tear slipping down her cheek. Six weeks they had waited for this day to come. "We'll be able to take the bandages off the week before Christmas," the doctor had said.

The door to the examination room swept open, and Dr. Harris came in. "Good morning, Mrs. Ellis," he said brightly. "How are you today?"

"Fine, thank you," she said. But she was too apprehensive for small talk.

Dr. Harris bent over the sink and washed his hands carefully. He was cautious with his patients but careless about himself. He could seldom find time to get a haircut, and his straight black hair hung a little long over his collar. His loosened tie allowed his collar to be open at the throat.

"Now then," he said, sitting down on a stool, "let's have a look."

Gently he snipped at the bandage with scissors and unwound it from Kenny's head. The bandage fell away, leaving two flat squares of gauze taped directly over Kenny's eyes. Dr. Harris lifted the edges of the tape slowly, trying not to hurt the boy's tender skin.

Kenny slowly opened his eyes, blinked several times as if the sudden light hurt. Then he looked at his mother and grinned. "Hi, Mom," he said.

Choking and speechless, the mother threw her arms around Kenny's neck. For several minutes she could say nothing as she hugged the boy and wept in thankfulness. Finally, she looked at Dr. Harris with tear-filled eyes. "I don't know how we'll ever be able to pay you," she said.

"We've been over all that before," the doctor interrupted with a wave of his hand. "I know how things are for you and Kenny. I'm glad I could help."

The mother dabbed at her eyes with a well-used handkerchief, stood up, and took Kenny's hand. But just as she turned toward the door, Kenny pulled away and stood for a long moment looking uncertainly at the doctor. Then he held his teddy bear up by its one arm to the doctor.

"Here," he said. "Take my Grr-face. He ought to be worth a lot of money."

Dr. Harris quietly took the broken bear in his two hands. "Thank you, Kenny. This will more than pay for my services."

The last few days before Christmas were especially good for Kenny and his mother. They sat together in the long evenings, watching the Christmas tree lights twinkle on and off. Bandages had covered Kenny's eyes for six weeks, so he seemed reluctant to close them in sleep. The fire dancing in the fireplace, the snowflakes sticking to his bedroom windows, the two small packages under the tree—all the lights and colors of the holiday fascinated him. And then, on Christmas Eve, Kenny's mother answered the doorbell. No one was there, but a large box was on the porch wrapped in shiny gold paper with a broad red ribbon and bow. A tag attached to the bow identified the box as intended for Kenny Ellis.

With a grin, Kenny tore the ribbon off the box, lifted the lid, and pulled out a teddy bear—his beloved Grr-face. Only now it had a new arm of brown corduroy and two new button eyes that glittered in the soft Christmas light. Kenny didn't seem to mind that the new arm did not match the other one. He just hugged his teddy bear and laughed.

Among the tissue in the box, the mother found a card. "Dear Kenny," it read. "I can sometimes help put boys and girls back together, but Mrs. Harris had to help me repair Grr-face. She's a better bear doctor than I am. Merry Christmas! Dr. Harris."

"Look, Mother," Kenny smiled, pointing to the button eyes. "Grr-face can see again—just like me!"

# *Christmas Prayer*

May the spirit of giving

Go on through the year,

Bringing love, laughter,

Hope, and good cheer.

Gifts wrapped with charity,

Joy, peace, and grace,

Ribboned with happiness,

A tender embrace.

Norma Woodbridge

# The Christmas Rose

By Lieutenant Colonel Marlene Chase

A light snow was falling as she turned the key to open Rose's Flower Shop. The name didn't take much imagination, but then it was better than "Rosie's Posies" as Clint had suggested when she had first begun business.

"Going to the Towers again this year?" asked Cass Gunther, who was opening the European deli next door.

Rose nodded. It was what they did every year. Supper and drinks at the club and Christmas Eve at the posh Park Towers. Swimming. The hot tub. Maybe take in a show. It was a tradition.

She turned on the lights, feeling bone tired. As usual, people waited until the last minute to place their Christmas orders. Why did she do this every year? It wasn't the money, though business had gone well. It filled her days, and there was something soothing about working with flowers.

"I'll be home for Christmas…" the sentimental lyric wafted from the radio under the counter. Home was four extravagantly decorated walls which she welcomed at the end of the day, but when it came down to it, what was there for

her really? Perhaps if they'd been able to have children. They'd had a reasonably good marriage, the best house on Carriage Drive, money in the bank, and enough friends to keep them from feeling lonely. And goodness knows they were too busy to think about whether or not they were happy. Bills for the mortgage, the car and boat and a half dozen credit cards never stopped.

Rose sighed. A hollowness plagued her. Even anticipating Clint's surprise when he would receive the Pendleton sport coat she'd bought held little joy. His gift to her would be something beautiful, expensive…but she couldn't remember last year's gift or when they had taken time to really talk to each other.

She felt suddenly at odds, cross. Perhaps if they'd kept up with the family. But family meant Clint's two aunts in Virginia and her stepfather in Wyoming, none of whom seemed famished for their company. Hungry, that was it. She'd forgotten to eat breakfast.

The bell over the door announced a customer, but she kept her back to the counter, consulting the order book.

"Excuse me, miss," an elderly voice called from behind her.

*I haven't been a miss in fourteen years, thank you.* She swallowed the caustic retort and turned slowly to find an old man smiling at her.

He had all his teeth, a look of kind apology and a full head of wavy white hair. He held a plaid cap across his chest and gave her a quaint little bow like an aging Sir Galahad. "I'm looking for some flowers—for my wife."

At those words, something luminous lit him from within. She wondered if Clint ever looked that way when he spoke about her. "I see," she said slowly, waiting.

He tapped gnarled fingers over his cap in meditation and with warm authority in his raspy voice said, "Not just any flowers. It must be Christmas roses."

"Well, we have roses. American beauty reds, pink, tea and yellow—"

"Oh, no," he said, shifting his negligible weight from one foot to the other. "Christmas roses—white as snow—with some of that feathery fern tucked in. And I'd like a big red bow, too."

"It's Christmas Eve, sir, and I'm afraid we're fresh out—"

"My wife loves white roses," he continued, looking at something she couldn't see. "They remind her of the Babe of Christmas and the purity of His heart. She hasn't seen any roses for

such a long time. And now that—"

The old man's shoulders drooped ever so slightly, then straightened again. Rose heard the faint tremor and was touched by something beautiful in the old face that made her think of alabaster. No, alabaster was too cold.

"She's ill now…" He paused and tucked his cap under his arm. "We served at a medical clinic in West Africa for more than thirty years. But we've had to return home. Nell has Alzheimer's. We're living at Country Gardens—"

"Oh, I'm sorry," Rose breathed.

The man rushed on without a trace of bitterness. "I have a little room on the floor just below the nursing wing where Nell is. We share meals together—and we have our memories. God has been good to us."

Rose returned his smile, uncomprehending, but unable to deny the man's sincerity. White roses on Christmas Eve? She might be able to get them from Warrensville, but it would be a stretch.

"We'll be spending Christmas Eve in my room—just the two of us—a celebration," he was saying. "Christmas roses for Nell would make it perfect."

"I may be able to get them sent over from Warrensville—" Rose bit her lip. *Was she crazy? It would take a miracle. Then there was the price.* "How much do you want to spend?"

The man set his cap on the counter and dug out a faded wallet from trousers that had seen several winters. He pushed four five-dollar bills toward her with childlike eagerness, then seeing her dismay, hesitated. "I hope it's enough."

"I could give you a nice spray of red roses in a bud vase," Rose began. *White rose centerpieces would start at thirty-five dollars. Then the delivery charge would run another twenty, especially on Christmas Eve. If she could get them!*

"I had hoped for a real special bouquet—" he broke off, and she read his profound disappointment.

"Leave it to me. I'll do my best to get you something nice," she began, astounded by her own words.

"Bless you!" the old man said, reaching across the counter and grasping her hands. "Can they be delivered around four or five? It will be such a surprise! I can't thank you enough." Nearly dancing, he replaced his cap and began backing toward the door. "Arnold Herriman— Room seven! Merry Christmas! God bless you! God bless you!"

What had a tired old man with a sick wife have to be so happy about? She puzzled over that through the next few orders, then placed a call to a supplier in Warrensville. They could get her a dozen white roses at $42.50—but it would be four o'clock before they could be relayed to her shop.

"Okay," she said wearily, realizing that she herself would have to deliver the Christmas roses to Mr. Herriman. No matter. Clint would likely be delayed by a promising client.

The flowers arrived at ten minutes to four and Rose quickly arranged them in a silver bowl, tucking in the feathery greens and sprigs of baby's breath and holly. She secured a lacy red bow into the base and balanced it in one hand while locking the door with the other.

Country Gardens hardly resembled its name. Surely a couple who'd spent a lifetime healing the sick in an obscure village deserved better in the sunset of their years.

She found the residential wing and tentatively approached number seven. Arnold Herriman in the same old trousers and shirt with a crimson tie beamed at her. She entered a room with a few pieces of old furniture and walls bursting with  pictures and certificates. On the hall table was a crèche. *The Babe of Christmas and the purity of His heart,* Herriman had said.

A diminutive woman sat on the sofa with hands folded over a patchwork quilt on her lap. She had a translucent complexion and vacant blue eyes above two brightly rouged cheeks. A bit of red ribbon had been tucked into her white hair. Her eyes widened when she saw the flowers, then spilled over with tears.

"Nell, darling. It's your surprise—Christmas roses," Arnold said, placing an arm around the woman's fragile shoulders.

"Oh, how lovely!" Nell stretched out her arms, her face transformed in radiance. She rubbed one wrinkled cheek against the delicate petals, then turned a watery gaze on Rose. "Do I know you, dear?"

"This is the nice lady from the flower shop who made your bouquet," Arnold said.

"Can you stay for a while, dear?" she asked. "We'll be finished with our patients soon, and we'll take you to our house for tea."

"Oh, no—" said Rose.

Arnold touched his wife's shoulder. "The patients are all gone, dear. We're home, and it's Christmas Eve."

Rose's throat ached with unshed tears and the sense that something beautiful lived here from which she was excluded. Could it be that in living their lives for others these two old people who had nothing but each other and a bouquet of white roses had everything that was important?

Suddenly Nell plucked one of the long-stemmed white roses from the elegant bouquet and held it out to Rose. "Please, I have so many. You must take one for yourself!"

"Yes," Arnold said, taking the stem from his wife and pressing it toward her, "Thank you for all your trouble. God bless you."

She wanted to say that He already had, that bringing them the Christmas roses had made her happier than she could remember in a long time, that on this Christmas Eve she had learned something of the meaning of the holiday she had missed until now.

*Let us sit down, in the twilight, by the flickering firelight, and think over for a moment just how much we owe to others for whatever happiness we enjoy. Think a moment, think tenderly and lovingly.... Let this Christmas be one of happiness, and the New Year be radiant with hope and filled with the impulse of doing something for somebody every day.*

Joe Mitchell Chapple

# A Family for Freddie

By Abbie Blair
Reprinted with permission from
December 1964 *Reader's Digest*

I remember the first time I saw Freddie. He was standing in his playpen at the adoption agency where I work. He gave me a toothy grin. "What a beautiful baby," I thought.

His boarding mother gathered him into her arms. "Will you be able to find a family for Freddie?"

Then I saw it. Freddie had been born without arms.

"He's so smart. He's only ten months old, and already he walks and talks." She kissed him. "Say 'book' for Mrs. Blair."

Freddie grinned at me and hid his head on his boarding mother's shoulder. "Now, Freddie, don't act that way," she said. "He's really very friendly," she added. "Such a good, good boy."

Freddie reminded me of my own son when he was that age, the same thick dark curls, the same brown eyes.

"You won't forget him, Mrs. Blair? You will try?"

"I won't forget."

I went upstairs and got out my latest copy of the Hard-to-Place list.

Freddie is a ten-month-old white Protestant boy of English and French background. He has brown eyes, dark-brown hair and fair skin. Freddie was born without arms, but is otherwise in good health. His boarding mother feels he is showing signs of superior mentality, and he is already walking and saying a few words. Freddie is a warm, affectionate child who has been surrendered by his natural mother and is ready for adoption.

"He's ready," I thought. "But who is ready for him?"

It was ten o'clock of a lovely late-summer morning, and the agency was full of couples— couples having interviews, couples meeting babies, families being born. These couples nearly always have the same dream: they want a child as much like themselves as possible, as young as possible, and—most important—a child with no medical problem.

"If he develops a problem after we get him," they say, "that is a risk we'll take, just like any other parents. But to pick a baby who already has a problem— that's too much."

And who can blame them?

I wasn't alone in looking for parents for Freddie. Any of the caseworkers meeting a new couple started with a hope: maybe they were for Freddie. But summer slipped into fall, and Freddie was with us for his first birthday.

"Freddie is so-o-o big," said Freddie, laughing. "So-o-o big."

And then I found them.

It started out as it always does—an impersonal record in my box, a new case, a new "Home Study," two people who wanted a child. They were Frances and Edwin Pearson. She was fourty-one. He was fourty-five. She was a housewife. He was a truck driver.

I went to see them. They lived in a tiny white frame house in a big yard full of sun and old trees. They greeted me together at the door,

eager and scared to death.

Mrs. Pearson produced steaming coffee and oven-warm cookies. They sat before me on the sofa, close together, holding hands. After a moment, Mrs. Pearson began: "Today is our wedding anniversary. Eighteen years."

"Good years." Mr. Pearson looked at his wife. "Except—"

"Yes," she said. "Except. Always the 'except.'" She looked around the immaculate room. "It's too neat," she said. "You know?"

I thought of my own living room with my three children. Teenagers now. "Yes," I said. "I know."

"Perhaps we're too old?"

I smiled. "You don't think so," I said. "We don't either."

"You always think it will be this month, and then next month," Mr. Pearson said. "Examinations. Tests. All kinds of things. Over and over. But nothing ever happened. You just go on hoping and hoping, and time keeps slipping by."

"We've tried to adopt before this," Mr. Pearson said. "One agency told us our apartment was too small, so we got this house. Then another agency said I didn't make enough money. We had decided that was it, but this friend told us about you, and we decided to make one last try."

"I'm glad," I said.

Mrs. Pearson glanced at her husband proudly. "Can we choose at all?" she asked.

"A boy for my husband?"

"We'll try for a boy," I said. "What kind of boy?"

Mrs. Pearson laughed. "How many kinds are there? Just a boy. My husband is very athletic. He played football in high school; basketball, too, and track. He would be good for a boy."

Mr. Pearson looked at me. "I know you can't tell exactly," he said, "but can you give us any idea how soon? We've waited so long."

I hesitated. There is always this question.

"Next summer maybe," said Mrs. Pearson. "We could take him to the beach."

"That long?" Mr. Pearson said. "Don't you have anyone at all? There must be a little boy somewhere.

"Of course," he went on after a pause, "we can't give him as much as other people. We haven't a lot of money saved up."

"We've got a lot of love," his wife said. "We've saved up a lot of that."

"Well," I said cautiously, "there is a little boy. He is thirteen months old."

"Oh," Mrs. Pearson said, "just a beautiful age."

"I have a picture of him," I said, reaching for my purse. I handed them Freddie's picture.

"He is a wonderful little boy," I said. "But he was born without arms."

They studied the picture in silence. He looked at her. "What do you think, Fran?"

"Kickball," Mrs. Pearson said. "You could teach him kickball."

"Athletics are not so important," Mr. Pearson said. "He can learn to use his head. Arms he can do without. A head, never. He can go to college. We'll save for it."

"A boy is a boy," Mrs. Pearson insisted. "He needs to play. You can teach him."

"I'll teach him. Arms aren't everything. Maybe we can get him some."

They had forgotten me. But maybe Mr. Pearson was right, I thought. Maybe sometime Freddie could be fitted with artificial arms. He did have nubs where arms should be.

"Then you might like to see him?"

They looked up. "When could we have him?"

"You think you might want him?"

Mrs. Pearson looked at me. "Might?" she said. "Might?"

"We want him," her husband said.

Mrs. Pearson went back to the picture. "You've been waiting for us," she said. "Haven't you?"

"His name is Freddie," I said, "but you can change it."

"No," said Mr. Pearson. "Frederick Pearson— it's good together."

And that was it.

There were formalities, of course; and by

the time we set the day Christmas lights were strung across city streets and wreaths were hung everywhere.

I met the Pearsons in the waiting room. There was a little snow on them both.

"Your son's here already," I told them. "Let's go upstairs and I'll bring him to you."

"I've got butterflies," Mrs. Pearson announced. "Suppose he doesn't like us?"

I put my hand on her arm. "I'll get him," I said.

Freddie's boarding mother had dressed him in a new white suit, with a sprig of green holly and red berries embroidered on the collar. His hair shone, a mop of dark curls.

"Going home," Freddie said to me, smiling, as his boarding mother put him in my arms.

"I told him that," she said. "I told him he was going to his new home."

She kissed him, and her eyes were wet.

"Good-bye, dear. Be a good boy."

"Good boy," said Freddie cheerfully. "Going home."

I carried him upstairs to the little room where the Pearsons were waiting. When I got there, I put him on his feet and opened the door.

"Merry Christmas," I said.

Freddie stood uncertainly, rocking a little, gazing intently at the two people before him. They drank him in.

Mr. Pearson knelt on one knee. "Freddie," he said, "come here. Come to Daddy."

Freddie looked back at me for a moment. Then, turning, he walked slowly toward them; and they reached out their arms and gathered him in.

*May you have the greatest two gifts of all on these holidays, Someone to love and someone who loves you.*

John Sinor

# A Christmas Gift I'll Never Forget

By Linda Deners Hummel

He entered my life twenty years ago, leaning against the doorjamb of Room 202, where I taught fifth grade. He wore sneakers three sizes too large and checkered pants ripped at the knees.

Daniel, as I'll call him, though that was not his real name, made this undistinguished entrance in the school of a quaint lakeside village known for its old money, white colonial homes, and brass mailboxes. He told me his last school had been in a neighboring county. "We were pickin' fruit," he said matter-of-factly.

I suspected this friendly, scruffy, smiling boy from a migrant family had no idea he had been thrown into a den of fifth-grade lions who had never before seen torn pants. If he noticed snickering, he didn't let on. There was no chip on his shoulder.

Twenty-five children eyed Daniel suspiciously until the kickball game that afternoon. Then he led off the first inning with a home run. With it came a bit of respect from the wardrobe critics of Room 202.

Next was Charles's turn. Charles was the least athletic, most overweight child in the history of fifth grade. After his second strike, amid the rolled eyes and groans of the class, Daniel edged up and spoke quietly to Charles's dejected back. "Forget them, kid. You can do it."

Charles warmed, smiled, stood taller and promptly struck out anyway. But at that precise moment, defying the social order of this jungle he had entered, Daniel had gently begun to change things—and us.

By autumn's end, we had all gravitated toward him. He taught us all kinds of lessons. How to call a wild turkey. How to tell whether fruit is ripe before that first bite. How to treat others, even Charles. Especially Charles. He never did use our names, calling me "miss" and the students "kid."

The day before Christmas vacation, the students always brought gifts for the teacher. It was a ritual—opening each department-store box, surveying the expensive perfume or scarf or leather wallet, and thanking the child.

That afternoon, Daniel walked to my desk and bent close to my ear. "Our packing boxes came out last night," he said without emotion. "We're leavin' tomorrow."

As I grasped the news, my eyes filled with tears. He countered the awkward silence by telling me about the move. Then, as I regained my composure, he pulled a gray rock from his pocket. Deliberately and with great style, he pushed it gently across my desk.

I sensed that this was something remarkable, but all my practice with perfume and silk had left me pitifully unprepared to respond. "It's for you," he said, fixing his eyes on mine. "I polished it up special."

I've never forgotten that moment.

Years have passed since then. Each Christmas my daughter asks me to tell this story. It always begins after she has picked up the small polished rock that sits on my desk and nestles herself in my lap. The first words of the story never vary. "The last time I ever saw Daniel, he gave me this rock as a gift and told me about his boxes. That was a long time ago, even before you were born.

"He's a grown-up now," I finish. Together we wonder where he is and what he has become.

"Someone good I bet," my daughter says. Then she adds, "Do the end of the story."

I know what she wants to hear—the lesson of love and caring learned by a teacher from a boy with nothing—and everything—to give. A boy who lived out of boxes. I touch the rock, remembering.

"Hi, kid," I say softly. "This is miss. I hope you no longer need the packing boxes. And Merry Christmas, wherever you are."

*O Father, may that holy Star*

*Grow every year more bright,*

*And send its glorious beam afar*

*To fill the world with light.*

William Cullen Bryant

# Sing a Song of Christmas!

Pockets full of gold;
Plums and cakes for Polly's stocking,
More than it can hold.
Pudding in the great pot,
Turkey on the spit,
Merry faces round the fire,
Smiling quite a bit!
Sing a Song of Christmas!
Carols in the street,
People going home with bundles
Everywhere we meet.
Holly, fir, and spruce boughs
Green upon the wall,
Spotless snow upon the road,
More about to fall.

Author Unknown

# Delayed Delivery

By Cathy Miller

There had never been such a winter like this. Stella watched from the haven of her armchair as gusts of snow whipped themselves into a frenzy. She feared to stand close to the window, unreasonably afraid that somehow the blizzard might be able to reach her there, sucking her, breathless, out into the chaos. The houses across the street were all but obliterated by the fury of wind-borne flakes. Absently, the elderly woman straightened the slip covers on the arms of her chair, her eyes glued to the spectacle beyond the glass.

Dragging her gaze away from the window, she forced herself up out of her chair and waited a moment for balance to reassert itself. Straightening her back against the pain that threatened to keep her stooped, she set out determinedly for the kitchen.

In the doorway to the next room she paused, her mind blank, wondering what purpose had propelled her there. From the vent above the stove the scream of the wind threatened to funnel the afternoon storm directly down into the tiny house. Stella focused brown eyes on the stovetop clock. The three-fifteen time reminded her that she had headed in there to take something out of the freezer for her supper. Another lonely meal that she didn't feel like preparing, much less eating.

Suddenly, she grabbed the handle of the refrigerator and leaned her forehead against the cold, white surface of the door as a wave of self-pity threatened to drown her. It was too much to bear, losing her beloved Dave this summer! How was she to endure the pain, the daily nothingness? She felt the familiar ache in her throat and squeezed her eyes tightly shut to hold the tears at bay.

Stella drew herself upright and shook her head in silent chastisement. She reiterated her litany of thanks. She had her health, her tiny home, an income that would suffice for the remainder of her days. She had her books, her television programs, her needlework. There were the pleasures of her garden in the spring and summer, walks through the wilderness park at the end of her street, and the winter birds that brightened the feeders outside her kitchen picture window. Not today though, she thought ruefully, as the blizzard hurled itself against the eastern wall of the kitchen.

"Ah, Dave, I miss you so! I never minded storms when you were here." The sound of her own voice echoed hollowly in the room. She turned on the radio that stood on the counter next to a neatly descending row of wooden canisters. A sudden joyful chorus of Christmas music filled the room, but it only served to deepen her loneliness.

Stella had been prepared for her husband's death. Since the doctor's pronouncement of terminal cancer, they had both faced the inevitable, striving to make the most of their remaining time together. Dave's financial affairs had always been in order. There were no new burdens in her widowed state. It was just the awful aloneness…the lack of purpose to her days.

They had been a childless couple. It had been their choice. Their lives had been so full and rich. They had been content with busy careers, and with each other.

They had many friends. Had. That was the operative word these days. It was bad enough losing the one person you loved with all your heart. But over the past few years, she and Dave repeatedly had to cope with the deaths of their friends and relations. They were all of an age—an age when human bodies began giving up—dying. Face it—they were old!

And now, on the first Christmas without Dave, Stella would be on her own. Mable and Jim had invited her to spend the holiday with them in Florida, but somehow that had seemed worse than staying at home alone. Not only would she miss her husband, but she would miss the snow, and the winter, and the familiarity of her own home.

With shaky fingers, she lowered the volume of the radio so that the music became a muted background. She glanced toward the fridge briefly, then decided that a hot bowl of soup would be more comforting fare this evening.

To her surprise, she saw that the mail had come. She hadn't even heard the creak of the levered mail slot in the front door. Poor mailman, out in this weather! "Neither hail, nor sleet…" With the inevitable wince of pain, she bent to retrieve the damp, white envelopes from the floor. Moving into the living room, she sat on the piano bench to open them. They were mostly Christmas cards, and her sad eyes smiled at the familiarity of the traditional scenes and at the loving messages inside. Carefully, her arthritic fingers arranged them among the others clustered on the piano top. In her entire house, they were the only seasonal decoration. The holiday was less than a week away, but she just did not have the heart to put up a silly tree, or even set up the stable that Dave had built with his own hands.

Suddenly engulfed by the loneliness of it all, Stella buried her lined face in her hands, lowering her elbows to the piano keys in a harsh, abrasive discord, and let the tears come. How would she possibly get through Christmas and the winter beyond it? She longed to climb into bed and bury herself in a cocoon of blankets, not emerging until her friends and spring returned.

The ring of the doorbell echoed the high-pitched, discordant piano notes and was so unexpected that Stella had to stifle a small scream of surprise. Now who could possibly be calling on her on a day like today? Wiping her eyes, she noticed for the first time how dark the room had become. The doorbell sounded a second time.

Using the piano for leverage, she raised herself upright and headed for the front hall, switching on the living room light as she passed. She opened the wooden door and stared through the screened window of the storm door with consternation. On her front porch, buffeted by waves of wind and snow, stood a strange, young man, whose hatless head was barely visible above the large carton in his arms. She peered beyond him to the driveway, but there was nothing about the small car to give clue to his identity. Returning her gaze to him, she saw that his hands were bare and his eyebrows had lifted in an expression of hopeful appeal that was fast disappearing behind the frost forming on the glass. Summoning courage, the elderly lady opened the door slightly and he stepped sideways to speak into the space.

"Mrs. Thornhope?"

She nodded confirmation, her extended arm beginning to tremble with cold and the strain of holding the door against the wind. He continued, predictably, "I have a package for you."

Curiosity drove warning thoughts from her mind. She pushed the door far enough to enable the stranger to shoulder it and stepped back into the foyer to make room for him. He entered, bringing with him the frozen breath of the storm. Smiling, he placed his burden carefully on the floor and stood to retrieve an envelope that protruded from his pocket. As he handed it to her, a sound came from the box. Stella actually jumped. The man laughed in apology and bent to straighten up the cardboard flaps, holding them

open in an invitation for her to peek inside. She advanced cautiously, then turned her gaze downward.

It was a dog! To be more exact, a golden Labrador retriever puppy. As the gentleman lifted its squirming body up into his arms, he explained, "This is for you, ma'am. He's six

 weeks old and completely housebroken." The young pup wiggled in happiness at being released from captivity and thrust ecstatic, wet kisses in the direction of his benefactor's face. "We were supposed to deliver him on Christmas Eve," he continued with some difficulty, as he strove to rescue his chin from the wet little tongue, "but the staff at the kennels start their holidays tomorrow. Hope you don't mind an early present."

Shock had stolen her ability to think clearly. Unable to form coherent sentences, she stammered, "But…I don't…I mean…who…?"

The young fellow set the animal down on the doormat between them and then reached out a finger to tap the envelope she was still holding.

"There's a letter in there that explains everything, pretty much. The dog was bought last July while her mother was still pregnant. It was meant to be a Christmas gift. If you'll wait just a minute, there are some things in the car I'll get for you."

Before she could protest, he was gone, returning a moment later with a huge box of dog food, a leash, and a book entitled *Caring for Your Labrador Retriever*. All this time the puppy had sat quietly at her feet, panting happily as his brown eyes watched her.

Unbelievably, the stranger was turning to go. Desperation forced the words from her lips. "But who…who bought it?"

Pausing in the open doorway, his words almost snatched away by the wind that tousled his hair, he replied, "Your husband, ma'am." And then he was gone.

It was all in the letter. Forgetting the puppy entirely at this sight of the familiar handwriting, Stella had walked like a somnambulist to her chair by the window. Unaware that the little dog had followed her, she forced her tear-filled eyes to read her husband's words. He had written it three weeks before his death and had left it with the kennel owners to be delivered along with the puppy as his last Christmas gift to her. It was full of love and encouragement and admonishments to be strong. He vowed that he was waiting for the day when she would join him. And he had sent her this young animal to keep her company until then.

Remembering the little creature for the first time, she was surprised to find him quietly looking up at her, his small panting mouth resembling a comic smile. Stella put the pages aside and reached for the bundle of golden fur. She had thought that he would be heavier, but he was only the size and weight of a sofa pillow. And so soft and warm. She cradled him in her arms and he licked her jawbone, then cuddled into the hollow of her neck. The tears began anew at this exchange of affection and the dog endured her crying without moving.

Finally, Stella lowered him to her lap, where she regarded him solemnly. She wiped vaguely at her wet cheeks, then somehow mustered a smile.

"Well, little guy, I guess it's you and me." His pink tongue panted in agreement. Stella's smile strengthened and her gaze shifted sideways to the window. Dusk had fallen, and the storm seemed to have spent the worst of its fury. Through fluffy flakes that were now drifting down to a gentler pace, she saw the cheery Christmas lights that edged the roof lines of her neighbors' homes. The strains of "Joy to the World" wafted in from the kitchen.

Suddenly Stella felt the most amazing sensation of peace and benediction washing over her. It was like being enfolded in a loving embrace. Her heart beat painfully, but it was with joy and wonder, not grief or loneliness. She need never feel alone again. Returning her attention to the dog, she spoke to him. "You know, fella, I have a box in the basement that I think you'd like. There's a tree in it and some decorations and lights that will impress you like crazy! And I think I can find that old stable down there, too. What d'ya say we go hunt it up?" The puppy barked happily in agreement, as if he understood every word.

*The heart hath its own memory, like the mind,*

*And in it are enshrined*

*The precious keepsakes, into which is wrought*

*The giver's loving thought.*

Henry Wadsworth Longfellow

# Long, Long Ago

Winds thru the olive trees

Softly did blow,

Round little Bethlehem

Long, long ago.

Sheep on the hillside lay

Whiter than snow,

Shepherds were watching them,

Long, long ago.

Then from the happy sky

Angel bent low,

Singing their songs of joy,

Long, long ago.

For in a manger bed,

Cradle we know,

Christ came to Bethlehem

Long, long ago.

Author Unknown

# A Bouquet of Hope

By Nancy Jo Sullivan

*I*t was a snowy, cold Christmas morning. The church was decorated with fragrant pine trees and cherry-red poinsettias trimmed with white lights. And it was crowded. My family and I took some of the few remaining seats in the front row. While I brushed the December snow from my boots, I saw Linda and Joe occupy the pew across from ours.

Linda and I had been friends for years. I knew that today the last place she wanted to be was in the front row with her sadness on display.

During the past four years, she and her husband had been struggling with infertility. Time and time again she had assured herself that a pregnancy would eventually happen. Wishing for a baby had become a burdensome cycle of building up hope, then surrendering unrealized dreams.

A few weeks earlier, around Thanksgiving, it seemed as if their dream of becoming a family would finally be realized. Linda and Joe had made preliminary arrangements to adopt a ten-month-old girl named Brianna.

It was to be an open adoption so Linda and Joe's social worker had arranged for them to meet Brianna's young, unwed mother at a local restaurant.

At the meeting, the young mother told her heart-breaking story of why she was releasing her little girl for adoption.

"I want you to have my baby," she told Joe and Linda

The next day, Brianna spent some time at Linda and Joe's home. For Linda, mothering Brianna felt natural; everything seemed so right.

The early weeks of December had passed quickly. Linda prepared for Brianna's arrival by buying diapers and baby clothes and a little stuffed doll. She even monogrammed Brianna's name on a Christmas stocking.

"It already feels like she's my daughter," Linda told me one morning as we sat at her kitchen table.

But just one week before Christmas, and only one night before Linda and Joe were scheduled to become legal guardians of Brianna, the social worker called with the news that the young mother had changed her mind.

Linda felt the all too familiar hopelessness as she hung up the phone.

Now as the church choir began singing the first verse of "Silent Night," I saw my friend wipe her eyes with the back of her hand.

After the service, Linda and I stood outside the church while our husbands scraped the snow from our cars.

"I feel like God is saying no," Linda said.

"Maybe He's not saying no." I reached for her mittened hands. "Maybe He's saying 'not yet.'"

A few days later I went to a floral shop seeking a gift of encouragement. A tall crystal vase filled with roses caught my eye. I was almost overcome with the beauty of the blossoms. Their soft, perfectly formed petals overshadowed the thorns of the long leafy stems, and they were a deep shade of red. It was refreshing to see something flowering in the middle of the winter.

"This is perfect," I thought as the florist took down Linda's address.

*If roses can bloom in December, so can hope,* I wrote on a small card.

When Linda received the bouquet, she called to thank me.

"Sometimes it's hard to hold onto hope," she admitted.

The winter weeks slowly turned into spring. Linda dried the roses and placed one in her favorite book of devotional prayers. The couple continued to seek a child to adopt, and daily Linda fingered the brittle, dry rose in her devotional book and prayed: *Lord, increase my faith…sustain my hope.*

Then one morning, Linda and Joe received a phone call from their social worker. "I have a young pregnant woman who is interested in you," the worker said.

Not long after the phone call, Linda dropped by my house. She was excited about the news, but hesitant.

"I *want* to have hope, but this feels so scary," Linda said.

I promised her my prayers.

Finally Joe and Linda received word that their birth mother was in labor. It was exactly one week before Christmas. Booking an early morning flight, Linda and Joe arrived at the

Arizona hospital in the late afternoon, just a few hours after the teenager had given birth to a healthy baby girl.

After signing papers that were needed for their part of the adoption, Linda and Joe watched the social worker knock on the birth mother's door; they still needed final signatures from her.

For nearly an hour Linda and Joe paced outside the room.

*Please, God, don't let her change her mind,* Linda prayed. She couldn't help but remember the last time she'd surrendered her dreams a year earlier.

At last the social worker opened the door and motioned the couple to join the birth mother and her new baby. "Everything is fine," the social worker whispered.

As Linda and Joe approached the bedside of the girl, they noticed how peaceful she looked. "She's always been your daughter." The teenager smiled and tenderly placed her baby in Linda's arms like she was presenting a priceless treasure.

Linda felt a strange mixture of sadness and joy. She felt compassion towards the mother as she imagined the grief of giving up a newborn baby. At the same time she felt unspeakable joy as she cradled the infant she would forever call her own.

Groping for words, Linda quietly stroked the face of her newborn daughter. "You've given us an amazing gift." Linda told the mother.

A few days later, a beautifully wrapped package arrived on my snow-covered doorstep. Taking the package inside, I pulled away layers of wrapping and found a dozen red roses. Attached was a message from Linda: *It's my turn to send the roses. This Christmas God sent me a beautiful bouquet...I'm holding her in my arms.*

*It came a flowerette bright, amid the cold of winter,
when half-spent was the night.
"Lo, How a Rose 'Ere Blooming"*

# A Kindled Flame of Love

Your friendship is a glowing

ember

Through the year; and each

December

From its warm and living spark

We kindle flame against the dark

And with its shining radiance light

Our tree of faith on Christmas

night.

Love so easily understands

What you can see is the smallest

part;

You don't need Christmas in your

hands

When you have Christmas in your

heart.

When it's Christmas man is bigger

and is better in his part;

He is keener for the service that is

prompted by his heart.

All the petty thoughts and narrow

seem to vanish for awhile

And the true reward he's seeking is

the glory of a smile.

Then for others he is toiling and

somehow it seems to me

That at Christmas he is almost

what God wanted him to be.

Edgar A. Guest

# The Christmas Nandina

## By Elizabeth Silance Ballard

*Nandina: "Nan-deena." An evergreen shrub with red berries and used by the Norbert family as a tabletop "Christmas tree." Paul Norbert*
*Nandina: "Nan-deena." A very lovely evergreen bush with red berries. It should stay in the yard and is definitely NOT a Christmas tree. Anne Norbert*

Anne and Paul had their first marital spat on December 15, three months after the wedding. Anne had been making exquisite lace ornaments for weeks and now she wanted to buy their first Christmas tree, a special tree, one they would always remember.

"But we already have our Christmas tree," Paul told her, and he went to the patio to get the nandina bush.

"A bush?" she asked, laughing, believing he must be teasing her. "A bush in a black plastic pot?"

But Paul was not teasing.

"The Norberts always have a nandina bush at Christmas. I guess I should have told you sooner, but it never occurred to me because it's just something we've done since I was twelve years old. It's our holiday tradition now and I won't change it."

Her face flushed. Oh, the nandina bush was pretty in its own way. It had been out on their patio since the day after their wedding when Paul had moved his things from the apartment he shared with his two brothers. Pretty as it was, though, it was not a Christmas tree. It was not something she wanted to place her lovely handmade ornaments on, and it would hardly hold even one string of the tiny white lights.

"But why?"

"Listen, Anne," he said. "Dad died when Davey was two years old and Mom did her best for the next three years. Then she got sick."

Anne listened as he went on to explain that his mother, Julia, had lost so many hours at the hosiery mill due to her illness that what little she had been able to provide for her three sons deteriorated rapidly. Mounting medical bills took priority as she tried desperately to get well.

"That was the first year we did not have a Christmas tree," Paul said, holding her close. "Randy was eight, Davey was five, and I was twelve—and disgusted. I wanted a Christmas tree. All my friends had one, and I was angry that we couldn't have one, too.

"A week before Christmas Mom came home from her doctor's visit and told me she needed surgery and that she would be going into the hospital on December 26. She said she had been hoping to work extra hours but she hadn't been able to do so."

"I'm going to need your help, Paul, to make Christmas special this year," she had told her oldest son.

Resentfully, Paul had listened to his mother's idea and helped her dig up the nandina bush from the yard and put it in a black plastic pot.

"I've always loved nandinas," she had said. "My grandmother had nandinas in her yard back in North Carolina, and there were always lovely red berries at Christmastime. See how many berries there are? They'll show up pretty if you and the boys put a few ornaments on it."

Paul thought of the tall trees with glittering ornaments and stars his friends had described, and the nandina bush seemed a poor substitute.

"We tried to decorate it to look like a real Christmas tree, and Randy and Davey thought it was great fun. Davey was too young to remember the Christmas trees we had in the past and Randy was always good-natured and eager to please so he didn't even question this strange substitute. No. I was the only one who hated the thing."

Julia had made it clear she understood Paul's anger and disappointment but she went on with her arrangements—packing a small bag for the hospital and trying to prepare food for them to have until she could get back home.

"On Christmas Eve morning we all walked the six blocks to church with us boys fussing when we had to stop several times to let Mom rest. When we finally reached the gray stone steps, she told me to stay outside with my brothers until she came back."

After a while Paul began to get anxious. People were arriving for the special children's service and to see the living nativity on the church lawn.

"My brothers were restless and started arguing, and I was worried that we would be late for the service. Besides, I was angry that I had been left outside with them so I went to find Mom."

Paul had wandered through the halls until he heard his mother's voice, talking softly and crying. It was something he had never seen his mother do.

"…and—well, if anything happens to me, my boys…"

Paul's heart pounded as he stood listening.

"My oldest one, Paul—well, he's had to help me so much since I've been sick. I really..,"

"It wasn't until then that I knew Mom was much sicker than I had realized and that she was very worried about us. I slipped back outside and told the boys that I couldn't find her, and when she came out she was smiling. Randy and Davey didn't even notice that her face was swollen and her eyes still teary, and we all went inside to the children's Christmas Eve service as if nothing were wrong."

Paul had no idea when they were delivered, but the next morning there had been several gifts piled on the table by the nandina bush. One for each of them from Julia and the others from their friends at church.

"There were two gifts for me," Paul said, smiling at the memory. "A Scrabble game and a book—a Hardy Boys mystery. I still have them."

Julia had lain on the sofa all smiles as the little boys screeched in the delight of ripping the bright wrapping paper. She had made their favorite breakfast—hot chocolate and monkey bread.

"Later in the morning, Randy's Sunday school teacher brought a huge tray of turkey, dressing, and a bag of other good things we had not eaten for a very long time. After Randy and Davey went to bed that night, Mom gave me pen and paper and asked me to write a thank-you note to our church who had provided for us on such short notice when she had been unable to do so herself.

"Mom went to sleep lying on the sofa, watching the tiny lights twinkle on the nandina bush while I sat at the kitchen table rewriting the thank-you note she had dictated so that it would be neat as she insisted.

"The next day she went to the hospital, and she never came home. That was the first Christmas 'tree' that Davey would remember, and it was the last one we had with Mom. We came to North Carolina to live with Aunt Violet who loved us and helped us through that first lonely, frightening year. Most of all she understood why, the following Christmas, we insisted on decorating the nandina bush we had brought from home.

"I love you, Anne, but in this one thing I won't give in."

Anne nodded, unable to speak, now seeing beyond the simple little bush to the love of a mother long departed who had left three sons behind, each possessing her quiet strength and tenderness. Julia had bequeathed to them a legacy of love, which now included Anne, and would include the children of Paul and Anne who were yet to come; children with whom they would share each year the story of the Christmas nandina.

*The most vivid memories of Christmases past are usually not of gifts given or received, but of the spirit of love, the special warmth of Christmas worship, the cherished little habits of the home.*

Lois Rand

# The Poinsettias

### By Louise Carroll

There were many poinsettia plants in church this year, and they were particularly full and deep red. As our Sunday school class was meeting before church, the topic of discussion was about these plants.

"Aren't they beautiful!" "This is the prettiest I've ever seen them." And then the question, "Why do we have poinsettias at Christmas?"

Millie said, "Because they look so nice." Anne said, "Because they look like Christmas—all red and green." Bill ventured, "Maybe some ancient superstition that has been forgotten." But most of the answers were, "I don't know." However, Aunt Jennie, who is wiser than the rest of us, said, "So God can use them to a good purpose."

At the Christmas Eve service, the poinsettias were placed across the front, on the lectern and on the windowsills. Certainly it seemed they had been put there to add beauty.

On Christmas morning, the poinsettias looked even more beautiful. Pastor McNulty announced to the congregation that those who had purchased the poinsettias should be sure to take them home after the service. But how was that he said it? "It would be a help to the ladies who are taking care of the plants if you would take your poinsettia home after the service."

Seven-year-old Bettie poked her sister, Bonnie, in the ribs and whispered excitedly, "Did you hear that? Did you? Did you? Now we have a Christmas gift for Mommy."

"Wow, Bettie, I prayed we would have a gift for Mommy."

Only a look from the kindly but stern-looking Miss Nelson quieted the two little girls. After the service, my friend, Ethel, was in charge of putting the poinsettias in plastic sleeves to protect them from the cold, bitter wind. As the crowd thinned out, two little girls approached Ethel. Ethel recognized Bettie and Bonnie as the daughters of Judy, a single parent who was going to school and working. Judy never came to church but she brought Bettie and Bonnie.

Bonnie, by virtue of being the oldest at eight years, spoke with assurance to Ethel, "We are going to give our poinsettia to our mother for Christmas."

It was a small church and Ethel was in charge of the poinsettias and so, although she kept careful notes, she was aware in her mind that neither Judy nor her children had purchased a poinsettia.

Ethel smiled and said, "I know your mother is going to be thrilled with such a nice gift."

Picking the fullest, reddest poinsettia she could find, Ethel lovingly slipped the plastic sleeve on it and handed it to Bonnie. Almost bouncing with excitement, the two little girls hurried out the door.

After everyone had left and Ethel was alone, she sat in the front pew a few minutes to think. There were still a few poinsettias left and on Monday she would deliver them to the nursing home.

How interesting, Ethel thought, Pastor McNulty hadn't made it clear about the poinsettias. It sounded as though there was one for everyone who wanted it.

Ethel smiled. Why do we put poinsettias in the church at Christmas? Just like Aunt Jennie said, "So God can use them for a good purpose."

# The Christmas Gift for Mother

In the Christmas times of long ago,
There was one event we used to know
   That was better than any other;
It wasn't the toys that we hoped to get,
But the talks we had—and I hear them yet—
   Of the gift we'd buy for Mother.

If ever love fashioned a Christmas gift,
Or saved its money and practiced thrift,
   'Twas done in those days, my brother—
Those golden times of Long Gone By,
Of our happiest years, when you and I
   Talked over the gift for Mother.

We hadn't gone forth on our different ways
Nor coined our lives into yesterdays
   In the fires that smelt and smother,
And we whispered and planned in our youthful glee
Of that marvelous "something" which was to be
   The gift of our hearts to Mother.

It had to be all that our purse could give,
Something she'd treasure while she could live,
   And better than any other.
We gave it the best of our love and thought,
And, Oh, the joy when at last we'd bought
   That marvelous gift for Mother!

Now I think as we go on our different ways,
Of the joy of those vanished yesterdays.
   How good it would be, my brother,
If this Christmas-time we could only know
That same sweet thrill of the Long Ago
   When we shared in the gift for Mother.

Edgar A. Guest

# Christmas Eve

*Christmas Eve...the night for which one lived all year...
yes, it was magic. The snow piled against the window
was not like other snows. The wind in the chimney
was not like other winds. If you scratched a frosted
place out of which to look, you saw the snow-packed
prairie to the north was a white country in which
no other person lived, that the snowpacked
timberland to the south was a white woods
forever silent. It was as though there
were no humans at all in any direction
but your own family. Christmas Eve
was a white that drew a
magic circle around the
members of your own family
to hem them all in and
fasten them together.*

Bess Streeter Aldrich

# A Little Christmas Story

## By Patricia Lorenz

After twenty years of driving buses for the Milwaukee county transit system, John thought he'd seen everything. But something happened one bitter, cold December day in Milwaukee that changed all that.

John was worrying about his problems just like the next guy. Wondering how he was going to pay the December gas bill. Wondering if he'd be able to buy any Christmas presents that year. Wondering if he was ever going to get ahead of the game.

On that cold, dreary, gray-sky day just before Christmas, the temperature was ten degrees and it was trying to snow. Every time John opened the bus door a blast of cold air slapped him in the face.

"Lousy time of year," John grumbled to no one in particular, "just plain lousy."

Around 3 P.M., John was driving his bus down Wisconsin Avenue through the heart of the city. At one of Milwaukee's private high schools he picked up the usual group of students.

The older boys pushed and shoved their way to the back of the bus. Then Frank, one of the younger kids, got on with a cheery, "Hi John" to the bus driver. Frank found a seat about four rows from the front.

The older boys in the back shouted and cracked jokes and it seemed to John that as Christmas drew closer they grew louder and more rowdy. *Rich kids,* John mumbled to himself disgustedly. Most of the boys from the prep school lived in the ritzier suburbs and would be transferring off his bus in a mile or so.

A few stops later, John pulled up in front of the Milwaukee County Medical Complex grounds where a woman was waiting in the bus shelter. She looked about forty years old, pregnant, and her dingy gray coat was tattered from collar to hem. When she pulled herself up the steps of the bus, John noticed she was only wearing socks, no shoes.

"Good Lord, woman, where are your shoes?" he blurted out without thinking. "It's too cold to be out without shoes! Get on in here and off that cold sidewalk!"

The woman struggled up the steps, pulling her gray buttonless coat around her protruding belly. "Never mind my shoes. This bus goin' downtown?"

Still staring at her feet John answered, "Well, eventually we'll get back downtown. Have to head west first, then we'll turn around."

"I don't mind the extra ride, long ás I can get warm. Lordy, it's cold out there. Wind must be comin' off the lake!" She sighed as she dropped her quarters into the fare box then plopped down onto the empty front seat.

The high school kids in the back started in.

"Hey lady, nice coat!"

"Must be from Saks Fifth Avenue, eh?"

"Hey, doesn't she know we don't serve patrons without shoes?"

John couldn't take it anymore. "That's enough, guys! Where's your manners?"

John felt like strangling every one of those kids. To distract the woman from their remarks, he continued his conversation, "Yup, it's a rough time of year all right."

The woman sat up straight in her seat and smoothed the wrinkles in her coat. "Sure is. I got eight kids. Had enough money this year to buy shoes for every one of 'em but that was it. I got some slippers at home but I didn't want to get 'em all wet in case it snowed."

John kept the conversation going. "Yep. It ain't easy with Christmas and all. Money's scarce. And if this weather doesn't warm up I'm wonderin' if I'll have enough to pay the gas bill."

"Mister, you just be glad you got a place to live and a job. The good Lord will take care of you. Always has for me."

John couldn't believe that a woman who didn't have any shoes was telling *him* to stop worrying.

Before long the bus was at the end of the line, time for the kids to get off and transfer to other buses that would take them to their comfortable suburban homes.

After the big boys filed off, Frank made his way up to the front, stopped next to the woman in the gray tattered coat and handed her his brand–new leather sport shoes.

"Here, lady, you take these. You need 'em more than I do."

"Oh no, son, I couldn't. Your Momma'll be mad if you come home without your shoes."

"No, ma'am. It'll be okay. I got a job. Paid for 'em myself. You need shoes. Please take 'em. It's okay."

And with that, Frank, a fourteen-year-old kid, walked off the bus and into the ten degree day in his stocking feet.

There's more, much more, to Christmas

Than candlelight and cheer;

It's the spirit of sweet friendship,

That brightens all the year;

It's thoughtfulness and kindness,

It's hope reborn again,

For peace, for understanding

And for goodwill to men!

Author Unknown

# Christmas Day in the Morning

By Pearl S. Buck

He waked suddenly and completely. It was four o'clock, the hour at which his father had always called him to get up and help with the milking. Strange how the habits of his youth clung to him still! Fifty years ago, and his father had been dead for thirty years, and yet he waked at four o'clock in the morning. He had trained himself to turn over and go to sleep, but this morning, because it was Christmas, he did not try to sleep. He slipped back in time, as he did so easily nowadays. He was fifteen years old and still on his father's farm. He loved his father. He had not known it until one day a few days before Christmas, when he overheard what his father was saying to his mother.

"Mary, I hate to call Rob in the mornings. He's growing so fast, and he needs his sleep. If you could see how he sleeps when I go in to wake him up! I wish I could manage alone."

"Well, you can't, Adam." His mother's voice was brisk. "Besides, he isn't a child anymore. It's time he took his turn."

"Yes," his father said slowly. "But I sure do hate to wake him."

When he heard those words, something in him woke: his father loved him! He had never thought of it before, taking for granted the tie of their blood. Neither his father nor his mother talked about loving their children—they had no time for such things. There was always so much to do on a farm.

Now that he knew his father loved him, there would be no more loitering in the mornings and having to be called again. He got up after that, stumbling with sleep, and pulled on his clothes, his eyes shut, but he got up.

And then on the night before Christmas, that year when he was fifteen, he lay for a few minutes thinking about the next day. They were poor, and most of the excitement was in the turkey they had raised themselves and in the mince pies his mother made. His sisters sewed presents and his mother and father always bought something he needed, not only a warm jacket, maybe, but something more, such as a book. And he saved and bought them each something, too.

He wished, that Christmas he was fifteen, he had a better present for his father. As usual, he had gone to the ten-cent store and bought a tie. It had seemed nice enough until he lay thinking the night before Christmas, and then he wished that he had heard his father and mother talking in time for him to save for something better.

He lay on his side, his head supported by his elbow, and looked out of his attic window. The stars were bright, much brighter than he ever remembered them being, and one was so bright he wondered if it were really the star of Bethlehem.

"Dad," he had once asked when he was a little boy, "what is a stable?"

"It's just a barn," his father had replied, "like ours."

Then Jesus had been born in a barn, and to a barn the shepherds and the Wise Men had come, bringing their Christmas gifts!

The thought struck him like a silver dagger. Why should he not give his father a special gift, too, out there in the barn? He could get up early, earlier than four o'clock, and he could creep into the barn and get all the milking done. He'd do it alone, milk and clean up, and then when his father went in to start the milking, he'd see it all done. And he would know who had done it.

At a quarter to three, he got up and put on his clothes. He crept downstairs, careful of the creaky boards, and let himself out. The big star hung lower over the barn roof, a reddish gold. The cows looked at him, sleepy and surprised.

"So, boss," he whispered. They accepted him placidly, and he fetched some hay for each cow and then got the milking pail and the big milk cans.

He had never milked all alone before, but it seemed almost easy. He kept thinking about his father's surprise. His father would come in and call him, saying that he would get things started while Rob was getting dressed. He'd go to the barn, open the door, and then he'd go to get the two big empty milk cans. But they wouldn't be waiting or empty; they'd be standing in the milk house filled…a gift to his father who loved him. He finished, the two milk cans were full, and he covered them and closed the milk house door carefully, making sure of the latch. He put the stool in its place by the door and hung up the clean milk pail. Then he went out of the barn and barred the door behind him.

Back in his room, he had only a minute to pull off his clothes in the darkness and jump into bed, for he heard his father up. He put the covers over his head to silence his quick breathing. The door opened.

"Rob!" his father called. "We have to get up, son, even if it is Christmas."

"Aw-right," he said sleepily.

"I'll go on out," his father said. "I'll get things started."

The door closed and he lay still, laughing to himself. In just a few minutes his father would know. His dancing heart was ready to jump from his body.

The minutes were endless—ten, fifteen, he did not know how many—and he heard his father's steps again. The door opened and he lay still.

"Rob!"

"Yes, Dad—"

His father was laughing, a queer sobbing sort of laugh. "Thought you'd fool me did you?" His father was standing beside him, pulling away the cover.

"It's for Christmas, Dad!"

He found his father and clutched him in a great hug. He felt his father's arms go around him. It was dark, and they could not see each other's faces.

"Son, I thank you. Nobody ever did a nicer thing—"

"Oh, Dad, I want you to know—I do want to be good!" The words broke from him of their own will. He did not know what to say. His heart was bursting with love.

"Well, I reckon I can go back to bed and sleep," his father said after a moment. "No, hark—the little ones are waked up. Come to think of it, son, I've never seen you children when you first saw the Christmas tree. I was always in the barn. Come on!"

Rob got up and pulled on his clothes again, and they went down to the Christmas tree; and soon the sun was creeping up where the star had been. Oh, what a Christmas, and how his heart had nearly burst again with shyness and pride as his father told his mother and made the younger children listen about how he, Rob, had gotten up all by himself.

"The best Christmas gift I ever had and I'll remember it, son, every year on Christmas morning, so long as I live."

They both remembered it, and now that his father was dead he remembered it alone: that blessed Christmas dawn when, alone with the cows in the barn, he had made his first gift of true love.

*Running to the window, he opened it, and put out his head. No fog, no mist; clear, bright, jovial, stirring, cold cold, piping for the blood to dance to, Golden sunlight; Heavenly sky, sweet fresh air, merry bells. Oh glorious! Glorious! Christmas Day!*

**Charles Dickens**

# Grandpa's Old-Time Christmas

Grandpa told me all about the old-time Christmas he had
When he was but six or eight, and just a teenie-weenie lad;
Said they didn't have much candy, and not very many toys,
But I bet he had a good time with the little girls and boys.
Christmas Eve he'd hang his stocking by the old-time chimney place,
Then he'd scamper up the stairway, crawl in bed and hide his face,
For he knew Old Santa wouldn't bring his reindeer o'er the snow
If a little boy could see him—everybody told him so.
Then next morning how he'd hurry down to see the things he had.
Things old Santa Claus had brought him, just to make a wee boy glad!
But in those days Santa didn't carry in his shoulder pack
Nice toys like my little train that runs along a little track;
Maybe there would be a little sheep on a wheel and painted white,
Maybe just a little tin bank that would hold his pennies tight,
And a little pair of mittens, and a pretty "nubia," too,
That would keep him warm and cozy when the winds of winter blew.
And they'd have a family dinner (all the relatives would meet,
Uncles, aunts, and lots of cousins), with such good things there to eat!
In the afternoon were walnuts, hickory nuts, and apples red,
And the kids would wrap up warm and slide down hill on grandpa's sled,
And there was the old melodeon that was played by Auntie Sue—
Little pedals worked the bellows, which was old and leaky too;
"Shall We Gather at the River?" they would sing, and "Happy Day."
And they'd bow their heads in silence while my grandpa's pa would pray.
Then he'd get the children 'round him so that all of them could hear,
And he'd tell of Jesus' birthday that we celebrate each year—
Tell the story of the Wise Men, and the star that led them on,
How they found Him in the manger, God's own well-beloved Son.
Oh, how grandpa's eyes would sparkle as he told of long ago,
When his hair was curly golden, though it now is white as snow!
When he'd finished, then he told me how to make my Christmas Best;
"Let your heart be filled with love, and that will outweigh all the rest."

*Charles Frederick Wadsworth*

# 365 Hours

The greatest gift I ever received was a gift I got one Christmas when my dad gave me a small box. Inside was a note saying, "Son, this next year I will give you 365 hours, an hour every day after dinner." My dad not only kept his promise, but every year he renewed it and it's the greatest gift I ever had in my life.

Author Unknown

...And it was always said of him, that he knew how to keep Christmas well, if any man alive possessed the knowledge. May that be truly said of us, and all of us!

Charles Dickens, *A Christmas Carol*

Christmas with us soon will be,

Holly, mirth, and gaiety;

Relatives we love we'll see.

In the children's games we'll find

Something to recall to mind

Things, with youth, we left behind.

May we from our plenteous store,

Aged and helpless cheer once more,

Send them happy from our door.

L. Lander

# A Treasure to Remember

By George Parler

*I*t was our turn to open our presents this particular Christmas morning. The living room was already covered with torn wrapping paper from the onslaught of the children's eagerness to unveil the hidden treasures that had tormented them for nearly a month. Now we adults sat around the room with our presents at our feet, slowly removing the paper while at the same time holding back the child within ourselves and maintaining our dignity in front of each other.

My wife, Brenda, and her family have a tradition of getting each other gag gifts. This always makes me a bit uneasy at Christmas or my birthday, never knowing what form of embarrassment lies waiting for me under the thin confines of the wrapping paper.

One of my daughters, Christy, who at the time was six years old, was standing directly in front of me. The excitement of the moment just beamed across her face. It was everything she could do to keep herself from helping me rip the paper from each present. Finally, I came to the last gift. And with my natural Sherlock Holmes ability, I deduced that this had to be the gag gift. Because with them it was never a question of "if," it was a question of when you came to it. So, with everyone looking on, I decided to go ahead and get it over with—just let them have their laugh—and I ripped off the paper.

And there it was…a toy airplane about two inches long. Our holiday guests started giggling to themselves as I looked up to my wife with a smirk on my face and blurted out, "A toy airplane, give me a break!"

Brenda gave me the look—that look that always tells me I have just put my foot in my mouth and am in the process of thoroughly chewing it. I had failed to look at the name tag before I opened the present to see who it was from. As I picked up the paper from the floor and read the name tag, my heart sank. On the tag were scribbled block letters that read, "To Dad, Love Christy." I have never felt as low at any time in my life as I did at that moment. One of the most agonizing experiences of my life was having to look down into her little face to find the joy that had once been there replaced with a look of total embarrassment and humiliation. The fear in her eyes spoke her thoughts of hoping no one would find out that the gift her father found so repulsive had come from her.

This loving child had taken her spending money that she could have spent on herself, but she had chosen instead to buy her daddy a Christmas present. And it wasn't just *any* present. She knew from watching me play computer video flight-simulator games that I was fascinated with airplanes.

I quickly knelt down and grabbed her up in my arms and held her as tight as I possibly could, willing to give anything to be able to take back those words. I made a feeble attempt to explain that I thought it had come from Mom, but since I found out it came from her, that made it different. It was obvious that nothing I could say was going to change the hurt in her little heart. I had to find a way to prove I meant what I said.

And I did. I took that toy airplane in my hand and began making airplane noises. I taxied onto the runway, which was the counter, and throttled to full thrust and was soon airborne. My mission goal was to remove the hurt from my baby's face—that I had caused—and to continue until her smile returned. I played all day with that airplane. I put so much excitement into that airplane that the other children left their new Christmas toys and wanted a turn playing with my little two-inch airplane. And just like a little selfish kid I said, "No, this is mine!" It wasn't very long until Christy's face was beaming with a smile again. But I didn't stop there. That little plane became a treasure of great wealth to me, and still is, for I still have that little two-inch plane.

I keep that plane mainly because it came from my little girl's heart with love. But it's also a reminder to me of the power of words.

*Let kindness come with every gift and good desires with every greeting.*

Henry Van Dyke

# Toothless Grin

## By Sharon Palmer

I was doing some last-minute Christmas shopping in a toy store and decided to look at fashion dolls. A nicely dressed little girl was excitedly looking through the same dolls as well, with a roll of money clamped tightly in her little hand. When she came upon a doll she liked, she would turn and ask her father if she had enough money to buy it. He usually said "yes" but she would keep looking and keep going through their ritual of "do I have enough?"

As she was looking, a little boy wandered in across the aisle and started sorting through some of the video games. He was dressed neatly, but in clothes that were obviously rather worn, and wearing a jacket that was probably a couple of sizes too small. He, too, had money in his hand, but it looked to be no more than five dollars or so, at the most. He was with his father as well, but each time he picked one of the video games and looked at his father, his father shook his head.

The little girl had apparently chosen her doll, a beautifully dressed, glamorous creation that would have been the envy of every little girl on the block. However, she had stopped and was watching the interchange between the little boy and his father. Rather dejectedly, the boy had given up on the video games and had chosen what looked like a book of stickers instead. He and his father then started walking through another aisle of the store.

The little girl put her carefully chosen doll back on the shelf, and ran over to the video games. She excitedly picked up one that was lying on top of the other toys, and raced toward the checkout after speaking with her father. I picked up my purchases and got in line behind them. Then, much to the little girl's obvious delight, the little boy and his father got in line behind me.

After the toy was paid for and bagged, the little girl handed it back to the cashier and whispered something in her ear. The cashier smiled and put the package under the counter. I paid for my purchases and was rearranging things in my purse when the little boy came up to the cashier.

The cashier rang up his purchases and then said, "Congratulations, you have been selected to win a prize!" With that, she handed the little boy the video game, and he could only stare in disbelief. It was, he said, exactly what he had wanted!

The little girl and her father had been standing at the doorway during all of this, and I saw the biggest, prettiest, toothless grin on that little girl that I have ever seen in my life. Then they walked out the door, and I followed, close behind them.

As I walked back to my car, in amazement over what I had just witnessed, I heard the father ask his daughter why she had done that. I'll never forget what she said to him. "Daddy, didn't Nana and PawPaw want me to buy something that would make me happy?" He said, "Of course they did, honey." To which the little girl replied, "Well, I just did!" With that, she giggled and started skipping toward their car.

I had just witnessed the Christmas spirit in that toy store, in the form of a little girl who understands more about the reason for the season than most adults I know! May God bless her and her parents, just as she blessed that little boy, and me, that day!

*Somehow, not only for Christmas, but all the long year through, The joy that you give to others is the joy that comes back to you.*

John Greenleaf Whittier

The magi, as you know, were wise men—who brought gifts to the Babe in the manger. They invented the art of giving Christmas presents.

O. Henry, *The Gift of the Magi*

# Christmas Without Grandma Kay

## By Robin Jones Gunn

"OK," I agreed with my husband, Ross. "We'll invite your family here for Christmas. But you know it's going to be hard for everyone since your mom passed away."

"I know," he said. "That's why we all need to be together." I sort of agreed with him. But I know I couldn't take Kay's place as hostess. I was still grieving myself and didn't feel I could be responsible for the emotional atmosphere on our first holiday without her.

I made all the preparations—cookies, decorations, presents—then on Christmas Eve welcomed Ross's family with open arms as I braced myself for a holiday punctuated by sorrow. That evening at church, our clan filled the entire back section. Afterwards, at home, the kids scampered upstairs and Ross shouted, "Five minutes!" The adults settled in the living room and Ross began to read from Luke 2.

At verse eight, our six-year-old, Rachel, appeared at the top of the stair wearing her brother's bathrobe, a shawl over her head, and carrying a stuffed lamb under her arm. She struck a pose and stared at the light fixture over the dining room table as if an angel had just appeared.

My father-in-law chuckled. "Look at her! You'd think she could really hear heavenly voices."

Next came Mary, one of my nieces who'd donned the blue bridesmaid dress I wore in my sister's wedding. I knew then that the kids had gotten into my closet. The plastic baby Jesus fit nicely under the full skirt of the blue dress. My son, appearing as Joseph, discreetly turned his head as Mary "brought forth" her firstborn son on the living room floor, wrapped him in a dish towel and laid him in the laundry basket.

We heard a commotion as Ross turned to Matthew 2 and read the cue for the Magi. He repeated it, louder: "We saw His star in the east and have come to worship Him."

One of my junior–high-age nephews whispered, "You go first!" and pushed his older brother out of the bedroom into full view. Slowly the ultimate wise man descended with Rachel's black tutu on his head, bearing a large bottle of canola oil.

The adults burst out laughing and I did too, until I realized what he was wearing. It was a gold brocade dress with pearls and sequins that circled the neck and shimmered down the entire left side. Obviously the kids had gone through the bags I'd brought home after we cleaned out Kay's closet. Bags filled with shoes, hats, a few dresses and some scarves that still smelled like her.

The laughter quickly diminished when my father-in-law said, "Hey! That's Kay's dress! What are you doing wearing her dress?"

Rachel looked at Grandpa from her perch at the top of the staircase. "Grandma doesn't mind if he uses it," she said. "I know she doesn't."

We all glanced silently at each other.

I didn't doubt that Rachel had an inside track into her grandma's heart. Kay had been there the day she was born, waiting all night in the hospital, holding a vase with two pink roses picked from her garden. She'd carried the roses through two airports and on the hour-long flight, telling everyone who she was going to see: "My son, his wife, my grandson and the granddaughter I've been waiting for."

I'd slept with the two pink roses on my nightstand and my baby girl next to me in her bassinet. When I awoke early in the morning to nurse my squirming, squealing infant, I noticed a red mark on her cheek. Was it blood? A birthmark I hadn't noticed before?

No, it was lipstick. Grandma Kay had visited her first granddaughter sometime during the night.

It was Grandma Kay who taught Rachel the three silent squeezes. A squeeze-squeeze-squeeze of the hand means, "I love you." My own introduction to the squeezes had been in the bride's dressing room on my wedding day. Kay slid past the wedding coordinator and photographer. In all the flurry, she quietly slipped her soft hand into mine and squeezed it three times. After that, I felt the silent squeezes many times. We all did. When we got the call last year that Kay had gone into a diabetic coma, Ross caught the next plane home. Our children and I prayed this would only be a close call, like so many others the past two years. But Kay didn't come out of it this time. A week later, we tried to accept the doctor's diagnosis that it was only a matter of days. The children seemed to understand that all we could do was wait.

One night that week, Rachel couldn't sleep. I brought her to bed with me but she wouldn't settle down. Crying, she said she wanted to talk to her Grandma.

"Just have Daddy put the phone up to her ear," she pleaded. "I know she'll hear me."

It was 10:30 P.M. I called the hospital and asked for Kay's room. My husband answered at her bedside. I watched my daughter sit up straight and take a deep breath.

"Okay, Rachel," my husband said. "You'll have to talk loud because there are noisy machines helping Grandma breathe."

"Grandma, it's me, Rachel!" she shouted. "I wanted to tell you good night. I'll see you in heaven."

Rachel handed me the phone and nestled down under the covers. "Oh," she said, springing up.

"Tell Daddy to give Grandma three squeezes for me."

Two days later, Grandma Kay died....

Now, on Christmas Eve, in our snow-covered house, Rachel was the first to welcome Grandma's memory into our celebration.

"Really, Grandpa," she continued to plead. "Grandma wouldn't mind."

We all knew Rachel was right. Grandma Kay wouldn't have cared if her grandchildren found delight in anything that belonged to her. If the dress had been embroidered with pure 14-karat gold, Grandma Kay wouldn't have minded a bit.

Grandpa nodded. The pageant continued. The next wise guy paraded down the stairs, stumbling on his too-big bathrobe and bearing a jumbo-sized Lawry's® Seasoned Salt. He laid it at the laundry basket.

My husband read about the shepherds returning, "glorifying and praising God for all the things they had heard and seen, just as they had been told."

Then the cast took a bow and scrambled for the kitchen where they fought over lighting the candle on Jesus' birthday cake.

When we started singing happy birthday to Jesus, I looked down at the little shepherdess standing next to me.

Rachel's small, warm hand nuzzled its way into mine. I knew Grandma Kay's memory would always be with us when I felt three silent squeezes.

*Those we hold most dear never truly leave us. They live on in the kindnesses they showed, the comfort they shared, and the love they brought into our lives.*

Isabel Norton

# Where's the Baby Jesus?

### By Jeannie S. Williams

Last December found me filled with the holiday spirit and doing some extensive, elaborate decorating. Our home was part of a Christmas open house tour sponsored by the women of our church to raise money for a local charity.

During the tour one person noticed the small nativity scene on my desk and admired its simplicity and loveliness. After examining it more closely, she noticed the empty manger and asked, "Where's the baby Jesus?"

Her question brought back memories of the year I purchased the broken nativity setting.

I was very bitter and disheartened that year because my parents, after thirty-six years of marriage, were getting a divorce. I could not accept their decision to part and I became depressed, not realizing they needed my love and understanding then more than ever.

My thoughts were constantly filled with childhood memories—the huge Christmas trees, the gleaming decorations, the special gifts, and the love we shared as a close family. Every time I thought about those moments, I'd burst into tears, being sure I'd never feel the spirit of Christmas again.

My children were afraid there wouldn't be any snow for the holidays that year, but two days before Christmas it began to fall. Beautifully and quietly it came during the morning, and by evening it covered everything in sight. I needed to go into town to buy some ribbon and wrapping paper, but I dreaded the idea. Even the new-fallen snow stirred memories of the past.

The store was crowded with last-minute shoppers—pushing, shoving, and complaining as they grabbed from shelves and racks not bothering to put unwanted articles in place. Christmas tree lights and ornaments dangled from open boxes, and the few dolls and stuffed toys reminded me of neglected orphans who had no home. A small nativity scene had fallen to the floor in front of my shopping cart, and I stopped to put it back on the shelf.

After glancing at the endless checkout line, I decided it wasn't worth the effort and had made up my mind to leave when suddenly I heard a loud, sharp voice cry out.

"Sarah! You get that thing out of your mouth right now!"

"But Mommy! I wasn't puttin' it in my mouth! See, Mommy? I was kissin' it! Look, Mommy, it's a little baby Jesus!"

"Well I don't care what it is! You put it down right now! You hear me?"

"But come look, Mommy," the child insisted. "It's all broken. It's a little manger and the baby Jesus got broked off!"

As I listened from the next aisle, I found myself smiling and wanting to see the little girl who had kissed the baby Jesus. I quietly moved some cartons aside and peeked through a space between the shelves. She appeared to be about four or five years old and was not properly dressed for the cold, wet weather. Instead of a coat she wore a bulky sweater several sizes too large for her small, slender body. Bright, colorful pieces of yarn were tied on the ends of her braids, making her look cheerful despite her ragged attire.

I continued to watch as she clutched the little doll to her cheek, and then she began to hum. Tears slowly filled my eyes as I recognized the melody. Another memory from childhood, a familiar little song: "Away in a manger, no crib for a bed, the little Lord Jesus lay down His sweet head." She had stopped humming and was softly singing the words.

Reluctantly I turned my eyes to her mother. She was paying no attention to the child but was anxiously looking through the marked-down winter coats displayed on the bargain rack near the end of the counter. Like her daughter she was rather shabbily dressed, and her torn, dirty tennis shoes were wet from the cold, melting snow. In her shopping cart was a small baby bundled snugly in a thick, washed-out, yellow blanket, sleeping peacefully.

"Mommy!" the little girl called to her. "Can we buy this here little baby Jesus? We can set Him on the table by the couch and we could…"

"I told you to put that thing down!" her mother interrupted. "You get yourself over here right now, or I'm gonna give you a spankin'. You hear me, girl?"

"But, Mommy!" exclaimed the child. "I bet we could buy it real cheap 'cause it's all broken. You said we ain't gonna get no Christmas tree, so can't we buy this here little baby Jesus instead? Please, Mommy, please?"

Angrily the woman hurried toward the child, and I turned away, not wanting to see, expecting her to punish the child as she had threatened. A few seconds passed as I waited tensely, but I did not hear a sound coming from the next aisle.

No movement, no scolding. Just complete silence. Puzzled, I peered from the corners of my eyes and was astonished to see the mother kneeling on the wet, dirty floor, holding the child close to her trembling body. She struggled to say something but only managed a desperate sob, and the little girl seemed to understand her despair.

"Don't cry, Mommy!" she pleaded. Wrapping her arms around her mother, she nestled her head against the woman's faded jacket and avidly apologized for her behavior. "I'm sorry I wasn't good in this store. I promise I won't ask for nothin' else! I don't want this here little baby Jesus. Really I don't! See, I'll put him back here in the manger. Please don't cry no more, Mommy!"

"I'm sorry, too, honey," answered her mother finally. "You know I don't have enough money to buy anything extra right now, and I'm just crying because I wished I did—it being Christmas and all—but I bet ol' Santa is gonna bring you them pretty little play dishes you been wantin' if you promise to be a real good girl, and maybe next year we can get us a real Christmas tree. How about that! Let's go home now 'fore Jackie wakes up and starts cryin', too." She laughed softly as she hugged her daughter and then kissed her quickly on the forehead.

The little girl was still holding the doll in her hands. She turned to put it on the shelf, glowing with anticipation. The possibility that Santa might bring her a set of dishes was all she needed to be happy once more.

"You know what, Mommy?" she announced excitedly. "I don't really need this here little baby Jesus doll anyhow! You know why? 'Cause my Sunday school teacher says baby Jesus really lives in your heart!"

I looked at the nativity scene and realized that a baby born in a stable some two thousand years ago was a person who still walks with us today, making His presence known, working to bring us through the difficulties of life, if only we let Him. To share in the glorious wonder of this holiday celebration and to be able to see God in Christ, I know one must first experience Him in the heart.

"Thank you, God," I began to pray. "Thank you for a wonderful childhood filled with precious memories and for parents who provided a home for me and gave me the love I needed during the most important years of my life, but most of all thank you for giving your Son."

I quickly grabbed the nativity scene pieces and hurried to the checkout counter. Recognizing one of the sales clerks, I asked her to give the doll to the little girl who was leaving the store with her mother, explaining I would pay for it later. I watched the child accept the gift and then saw her give "baby Jesus" another kiss as she walked out the door.

Once again the Christmas season will be approaching. Christmas—a time for rejoicing, a time for giving, a time for remembering!

The little broken nativity scene I purchased that evening graces my desk every Christmas. It's there to remind me of a child whose simple words touched my life.

*That night some shepherds were in the fields outside the village, guarding their flocks of sheep. Suddenly an angel appeared among them.... He said, "I bring you the most joyful news ever announced, and it is for everyone! The Savior has been born tonight in Bethlehem!"*

The Book of Luke

# A Christmas Prayer

Loving Father, help us remember the birth of Jesus, that we may

share in the song of the angels, the gladness of the shepherds,

and the worship of the wise men.

Close the door of hate and open the door of love all over the world.

Let kindness come with every gift and good desires with every greeting.

Deliver us from evil by the blessing which Christ brings, and

teach us to be merry with clear hearts.

May the Christmas morning make us happy to be Thy children,

and the Christmas evening bring us to our beds with grateful

thoughts, forgiving and forgiven, for Jesus' sake. Amen!

Robert Louis Stevenson

*A* happy, happy Christmas, be yours to-day! Oh, not the failing measure of *fleeting earthly pleasure, but Christmas joy abiding while years are swiftly gliding, be yours, I pray, through Him who gave us Christmas day.*

Frances Ridley Havergal

# Acknowledgments

A diligent search has been made to trace original ownership, and when necessary, permission to reprint has been obtained. If I have overlooked giving proper credit to anyone, please accept my apologies. Should any attribution be found to be incorrect, the publisher welcomes written documentation supporting correction for subsequent printings. For material not in the public domain, grateful acknowledgment is given to the publishers and individuals who have granted permission for use of their material.

Acknowledgments are listed by story title in the order they appear in the book. For permission to reprint any of the stories please request permission from the original source listed below.

*"Mrs. Hildebrandt's Gift"* by Robert Smith. Reprinted from the Feb/Mar 1994 issue of *Country* magazine. Used by permission of the author.

*"A Gift From the Heart"* by Norman Vincent Peale. Reprinted with permission from the January 1968 *Reader's Digest.* Copyright © 1968 by the Reader's Digest Association, Inc.

*"A New Way to See Christmas"* by Gary B. Swanson. Reprinted from the December 1997 issue of *Focus on the Family* magazine. Used by permission of the author.

*"The Christmas Rose"* by Lieutenant Colonel Marlene Chase © 1997. Excerpted from *The War Cry,* national publication of The Salvation Army. Used by permission of the author.

*"A Family for Freddie"* by Abbie Blair. Reprinted with permission from the December 1964 *Reader's Digest.* Copyright © 1964 by the Reader's Digest Association, Inc.

*"A Christmas Gift I'll Never Forget"* by Linda DeMers Hummel. Originally printed in *Family Circle* magazine. Used by permission of the author.

*"Delayed Delivery"* by Cathy Miller, originally from an article in *Northern Life,* Dec. 26, 1992. Quoted from *Christmas in My Heart,* Vol. 2 by Joe Wheeler, 1995. Cathy Miller lives in Sudbury, Ontario, Canada, where she teaches elementary school and continues to write in her spare time. Used by permission of the author.

*"A Bouquet of Hope"* by Nancy Jo Sullivan © 2000. Used by permission of the author.

*"The Christmas Nandina"* by Elizabeth Silance Ballard © 1998. Used by permission of the author.

*"The Poinsettias"* by Louise Carroll. As printed in *The Lutheran Digest.* Used by permission of the author.

*"A Little Christmas Story"* by Patricia Lorenz © 1985. Used by permission of the author. Patricia Lorenz is an inspirational, art-of-living speaker and author of two books, over 400 articles, hundreds of devotionals, and stories in nine Chicken Soup for the Soul books. For speaking engagements e-mail her at patricialorenz@juno.com.

*"Christmas Day in the Morning"* by Pearl S. Buck © 1955. Used by permission of Harold Ober Associates.

*"A Treasure to Remember"* by George Parler © 1996. Used by permission of the author.

*"Toothless Grin"* by Sharon Palmer © 1999. Used by permission of the author. Dedicated to my nieces, Rebecca, Erin, and Cassidy, whose hearts are big enough to do the same. Write to their "Auntie Beep" (me!) at Sharon-Palmer@mindless.com in Nashville, Tennessee.

*"Christmas Without Grandma Kay"* Robin Jones Gunn, © 1993. Condensed from *Virtue Magazine,* Nov/Dec 1993. Used by permission of the author. All rights retained.

*"Where's the Baby Jesus?"* by Jeannie S. Williams, © 1984. First published in *Vital Christianity,* December 1984. Used by permission of the author. All rights retained.